# The Autumn of Love

By Jim Wortham

Jim Wortham

James Wortham Publishing Company
P O Box 40
Madison, Indiana 47250-0040 U.S.A.

Email: JimWortham123@gmail.com

Autographed books may be ordered
direct from author.
See page 132 for order information.

**The Autumn of Love**

Art via Unsplash, Pixabay
Editor & Typesetter: Gypsy Mercer
Cover Design:  Gypsy Mercer
Excerpts by permission of author and publisher:
   **Searching for Someone/Jim Wortham**
   **Thinking of You/Jim Wortham**

*Author's note:  this is a work of fiction.  Names, characters, places and incidents are a product of the author's imagination.  Any resemblance to actual people, living or dead, or actual events is purely coincidental.*

**The Autumn of Love/Jim Wortham** ~ First Edition
ISBN 978-1928877219

Library of Congress Control Number: 2020918633

# <u>Dedication</u>

To all who cover my world with love
     and gentleness
To all who still believe in love
To those who are now in love
To those who were once in love
To all who have cried at night
     because of a love that ended
To friends who believed my dreams
     would come true

*Your encouragement*
*and friendship*
*turned my*
*dreams*
*into reality*

Jim Wortham

# Part One

people
are
fragile

HANDLE
WITH
CARE

Jim Wortham

# I WAS HOPING

I know
two weeks of love
is better than none

I was just
hoping
love would last
longer

## CLASSY WOMAN

You have a musical name
Maria
Your hair swings long
across your face
You are fun to look at
because of your big smile
and gentle eyes

You know all
the right words to use
to make a man feel fine
Never words to inflate an ego
just words to let him know
you like how he treats you
that you enjoy being with him

You are a classy woman, Maria
I want to know you better

Jim Wortham

# WHERE IS JOHNNY

Johnny was ugly
Most girls ignored him
when he spoke

The last time I saw Johnny
he was at a local joint
I watched twelve girls
turn him down
for dances

Then he left
walking away
fading into the night
into Nobody Cares Land

## QUICKLY

Our paths crossed
You needed comfort
I needed to care

My care
turned to love
Your need for comfort
disappeared

You moved
away from town
away from me

Our paths
separated quickly
just as they crossed

Jim Wortham

## <u>A POET'S PEN</u>

When love is over
words flow freely
from my pen

Why
I don't know
Perhaps I go into a deeper
level of thought
The level where I ask myself
why    why    why
?

A thousand whys
I ask myself
A thousand answers I receive
And the answers fall
into my pen

## <u>HOTEL</u>

In this

run down hotel

I eat

cheese

and

round Ritz crackers


No one is around

And it is

cracker crumb lonely

Jim Wortham

## <u>LOVE ME ANYWAY</u>

When you
know
     everything
     about
     me

Will
     y
     o
     u
love me then
     ?

## LOVE IS OVER

How do I say
that I have
no more love
to give you
?
How do I say
goodbye
when you still love me
more each day
?
How do I end something
that began too quickly
?

Jim Wortham

## GOOD-BYE

I must go
I am sorry
I must be alone at times
I need to be with others sometimes
You allow me
to do neither

If anything destroyed our love
it was not giving me freedom
I miss embraces with those
I like
I miss nights alone
for the sake of being alone
to think about yesterday's loves
and tomorrow's dreams

Good luck
Will we meet again
when we are both different
?

# LIFE IS FOR LOVING

Yes
I feel what you feel
I love as you love
I dream as you dream

You are beautiful
You are not convinced
that your dreams
are impossible to reach

Fly above your doubts and fears
Hold fast to your dreams
above all
love life
Even if you fall short of your dreams
Love what does come true
Love what you do become

Jim Wortham

## <u>UNLOVED</u>

I liked myself

until you
loved me
and left

Now
I doubt
myself
again

BOB

Bob j u m p e d

at stars

and d * a * n * c * e * d

under rainbows

He was a
beautiful
person

Surely
God cried
when the ocean
took him  unexpectedly

Jim Wortham

# <u>BOYS ARE AFRAID</u>

I see
girls
sitting on the beach

The girls
would like
boys to join them

but boys
are afraid
of
rejection

## <u>PEOPLE</u>

People
are afraid
to talk
with people

        There is
        so much love
        going
        to waste

Jim Wortham

# I NEGLECTED YOU

How was I to know
that one day
I would look up
and you would never
be there again
?

If I had known
I would have listened
to you laugh
and memorized every detail
about you

Instead
I read books
and listened to records
while you sat next to me
waiting

## <u>CANDY STORE</u>

A girl
smiled
from behind
a candy counter

We talked
and laughed
I wanted to leave
her something

so I gave her
a kiss

Jim Wortham

## <u>SANDWICHES</u>

Years ago
I dated a girl
who fixed sandwiches
for picnics

Girls now
take everything
I have
and ask for more

I am looking
for a girl
who will fix sandwiches
again

## <u>ALIVE</u>

Maria does not
wait around
for someone
to bring her
alive again

She goes out
and finds ways
to make herself
alive

Jim Wortham

# HAPPY TIMES

Happy times
are all
around us

       They only
       have to be
       discovered

## POPSICLES

Pretty girl
bring your
     popsicles
     cotton candy
into my world
I am tired of being serious
and I am ready to play

Let us sit on the sand
We will laugh
     swim
     exchange secret thoughts

We will dance on the beach
to the sounds of the ocean's breeze
Life is for having fun
Let us begin today

Jim Wortham

## UNAWARE

I am watching a girl
sitting on the grass
She has on a pop art dress
and wooden earrings
She seems unaware
of what is going on

She is about
seventeen years old
and very
very pretty

My mind goes back
to that time in my life
I realize now how
different life is
than what I believed so long ago

Silently (just to myself)
I ask the girl
how long will it be
until you marry and discover
your idea of love does not exist
?

And about that terrific job
you long for in the days ahead
How long will it be
until the cold world
shuns your talents
and gives you a simple job
of typing
or sweeping the floor
or worse
no job at all
        ?

In ten years
dear girl
you will be full of surprises
sad ones
I am afraid

This happened to me
But I am hanging on
still hoping to break
into that beautiful world
I always hoped was there
I believe if I try enough
and God hears my cry
life might be
something like
I believed it to be
all those years ago

Jim Wortham

## <u>LONELY WALKS</u>

Alone tonight
walking past
guys
and girls

No one
takes time
to talk

Part Two

games

p
e
o
p
l
e

play

Jim Wortham

# DO NOTHING

Sometimes
doing nothing
is
what I need to do

Sometimes
doing nothing
is all I need to do

Sometimes
doing something
is wrong

Sometimes waiting
for an answer
in silence
is the right thing to do

# I DO NOT WANT TO PLAY

I know
many games

that lovers
play
to cause
jealousy

With you
I hope
I can
put them away

Jim Wortham

## <u>SECRETS</u>

It was disappointing
to see it happen
She gave
all she had to give
to him

When there was nothing
more for her to give
he lost interest

## ACCEPT ME

Do not make me

live a lie


Accept me

as I am

Join me

or leave


Do not shame me

into putting

up defenses

or being phony

Jim Wortham

## <u>SKIP</u>

Girl
you laugh
and skip
But you are
afraid
to reveal
yourself

## SHE NEVER RETURNED

They took one another
for granted
because each
was always there

One day
it was not so
One was missing
and never returned

And the other
could not take it
even for granted

Jim Wortham

## POPULARITY

No one
liked her

One day
she became
popular in
one man's eyes

When that happened
everyone began
to like
her

## RISK

To speak
my thoughts
is a risk
I could lose you
if you are not ready
to hear them

Not to speak
my words
is also a risk
my thoughts
if spoken
might bring
us closer

Jim Wortham

# MENTAL JAIL

You are in a
mental jail
You have been imprisoned
by what you believe
others
might think about you

You cannot be yourself
You are afraid to
laugh
dance
sing

Fear has bound you
with tight chains
You are afraid
to be yourself

# WHAT HAPPENED

When I began
to love her
more


something
happened


She began
to
love me less

Jim Wortham

## EXPLOSION

She let her bottled
fears
anxieties
and imperfections
explode
For the first time
I saw her real self
I liked what I saw

It was too much
for her
to expose these imperfections
so she left

I thought her imperfections
were beautiful
but she did not
wait
long enough
for me to tell her

## ONCE UPON A YESTERDAY

Our story could have been
we lived happily ever after
but you would not
give us a chance

You wanted to fall in love
with everyone you met
Now
late in life
your hair graying
you ask to return
to the relationship
we once had

I cannot do it
I am
very sorry
for you

Jim Wortham

## <u>CARE FOR ME</u>

My mind

cries out

for someone

who will care

     and put

     selfishness

     aside

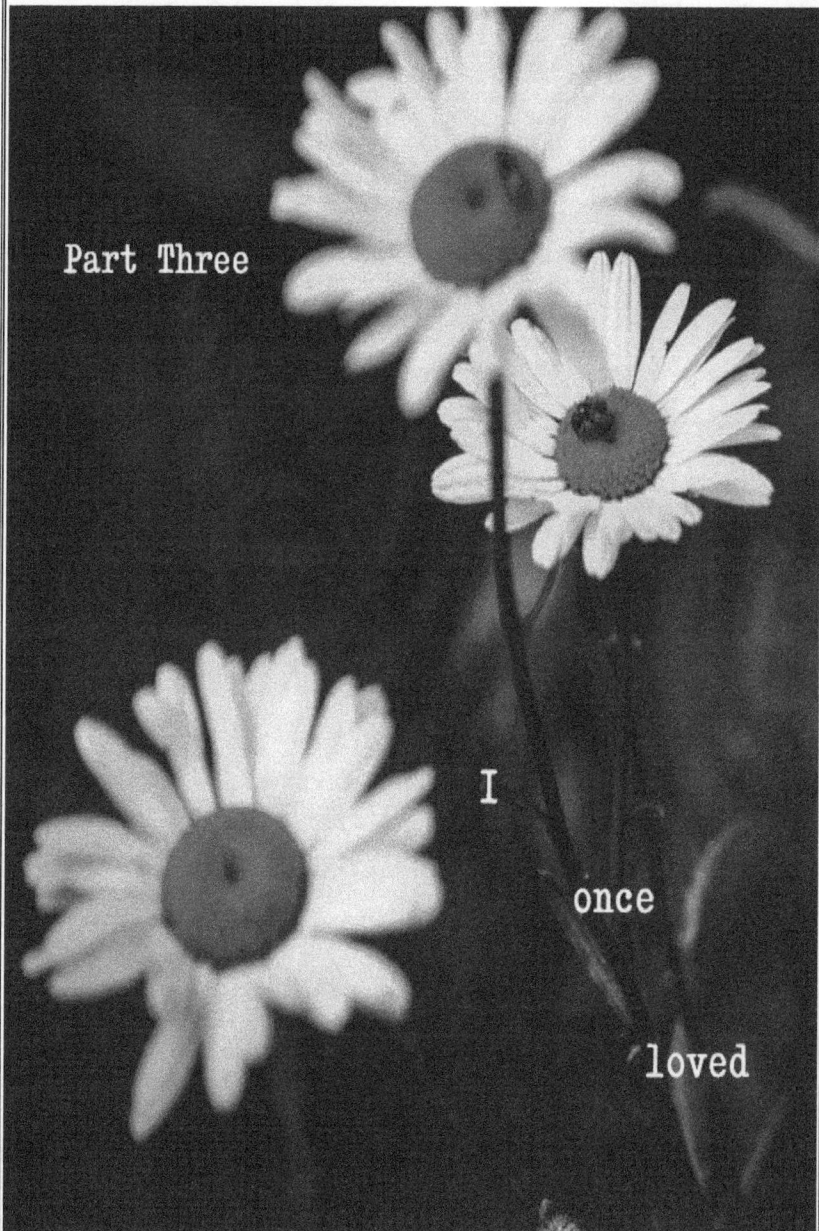

Part Three

I

once

loved

Jim Wortham

## LIGHTHOUSE

I leave the lamp on
next to my bed
I turn the music on
The lamp and the music
are my lighthouse
reminding me of the beacon
you cast
when I found your love
in the darkness
Now the beacon
is for you
Lighthouse
be my friend tonight

# I FIRST SAW YOU

I remember when I first saw you
I knew
We had the same sensitive spirit
Your eyes and expression told me
even before we spoke

I knew we would be
enjoying beautiful moments
together

My heart
began to beat loudly
Did you hear it
              ?

Jim Wortham

## <u>FRAGMENTS</u>

```
I put
  f
    r
      a
        g
          m
            e
              n
                t
                  s
of you
on paper

to capture
the
        m o m  e  n  t
we met
```

## IT EXCITES ME

Your hair

excites

me

The

way it is parted

the way it lays

on both sides of your face


It makes

you

look romantic

Jim Wortham

# INFATUATION

The infatuation
of meeting you
has entered
its second day


My mind
asks questions
like


What will
tomorrow be like
?
Will this infatuation
turn to love
?

## DELICIOUS PERFUME

You like
to try
new things with me

Today
you took a
bottle of vanilla
and splashed some
on your face
and down your neck

You invented
a new kind of
delicious perfume

Jim Wortham

# <u>FALLING</u>

Each

time


I discover

something new

about you


I fall

deeper

in love

I have been
counting the days
since you left

I believe it is
almost time
for love
to come again

Jim Wortham

# I AM FRAGILE

I will
seek out
the best in you
I will affirm
your beautiful qualities

I ask that you
look for the best
in me too
I am fragile
like you

Surround me
with an atmosphere
of love
and I will see
and correct my faults

## MARSHMALLOWS

I watch as you
burn marshmallows
on a stick
over a fire

I am glad you like
burnt marshmallows
I do too

For the longest time
I thought maybe
something was
wrong with me

Jim Wortham

## MAGIC OF LOVE

I thought it was magic
that kept me thinking about you
long after we were apart

Next time together
your eyes danced
You were dressed in cheerful colors
You told me about your God
with carefully laced words of love
As I listened to you
it seemed like the parties
with drinking and drugs
didn't matter anymore
I caught an idea
of someone else I could be

Someone confident
Someone with a purpose
Someone with joy and peace

It was because of what you were
and the love you showed
that I asked Jesus to change my
life
And he did

Jim Wortham

## <u>YOU ARE A DREAM</u>

It has always
been an impossible dream
to meet someone
who would love me as much
as I would love her

With you
I have given love
and have had love returned

It has taken
so many years
to find you

P L E A S E    S T A Y

## FOUNTAIN OF LOVE

You asked what I would do
when your beauty began to
fade from age
Let me assure you
My Love
that you are always beautiful
to me
I will give you nice presents
that I wrap myself
Love Touch cards
kisses and hugs
strawberry scented candles
sonnets of love and praise
to keep you young
I promise you
My Love
that as we walk down
life's path together
I will know
just what to give you
to keep you
young and beautiful

Jim Wortham

# <u>STEPPING INTO LONELINESS</u>

I had no idea
about your loneliness
How could I know
         ?

You were friendly
always offering a smile
and small talk

I knew some guys wanted
a relationship with you
but no one actually asked you
on a date

These guys seemed
afraid of rejection
No one asked for your
phone number

I started thinking
these guys are so shy
They are hoping you
would ask them on a date

One night
I passed a building
I thought was abandoned
until
I saw you unlock the door
walk up several flights of stairs
then a single light bulb
came on
It was the third floor

A television flickered on
You fell onto your couch
alone
no curtain over the window
the whole world saw
your loneliness

Jim Wortham

# TELL ME

Please tell me
If anything I do
causes you hurt
Please tell me

I want
our relationship
to become deeper each day

I cannot see past experiences
that have caused you pain
So I might cause you to feel insecure
without realizing it
because I do not know
you well enough

Care enough to tell me
your hurts when they arise
I will not laugh
I will weep with you
I will understand
and our relationship
will become deeper

## <u>SHELLS</u>

It amazes me
how you are never in a rush
We spent the day
on the beach

I watched you
gathering shells
When night came
you made them into
exotic earrings and necklaces

There are so many things
I don't know about you
and I want to spend
my entire life
discovering them

Jim Wortham

# <u>KISS ME, LOVE ME</u>

I treat you
with love and respect
My loving words are only
for you

I will love you forever
but
when my heart breaks
it will not heal
I will still want and love you

I love you now
I always will

Accept my love today
for all your tomorrows

Love me back
with all your tomorrows
I will pay with
a thousand kisses
for the memories
you leave

Jim Wortham

# CINDY, I LOVE YOU

I remember
how our eyes met
with anticipation

I remember
your bright red and blue jumpsuit
and golden earrings sparkling
under colored lights
the white belt
around your slim waist

I remember the ecstasy
of holding your hand
our lips touching

I remember days together
even your secret thoughts
I picked up
by knowing you so well

One night you called
Your parents were moving
to California

I remember your words
        I will write every day
        I will love you more each day
        Someday we will marry
I believed you

That was ten years ago, Cindy
Perhaps you forgot
how our eyes met at the roller rink
Perhaps you forgot you said
        I love you
But you will be remembered by me
and by all who read this poem

Jim Wortham

## <u>PORTRAIT</u>

Being aloof
is not
part of you

You let everyone
know you
like them

You are
a human
portrait of God

# SIMPLE LIFE

I chose
a simple life
I receive a few dollars
for a good poem

I live in an apartment
with posters
scented candles
bamboo hanging
from the ceiling

I own a car
old but it runs
My jeans are faded

I choose
a simple life
I am happy

Jim Wortham

# SEARCHING

I am thinking of
a beautiful woman
to keep me going
The one I might meet
someday

I look on college campuses
    on streets
    in parks
I always miss her

Sometimes I wonder
if she really exists
I mean
she exists
in my mind
but will I really
meet her someday
      ?

Sometimes I think
I have found her
but after
    talking
    laughing
    sharing
parts of our lives
entertaining each other
we always part as friends

Now life is moving on
and I wonder
if never meeting her
will keep me going

Jim Wortham

# TOO LATE

School pressures
brought out irritability
in me

One day
I was upset
I said something unkind
*(I did not mean it)*
It broke your heart
*(I am sorry I said it)*

You cried
*(then I cried)*

But it was too late
to stop your hurt
*(and stop the hurt I felt for you)*

It was too late

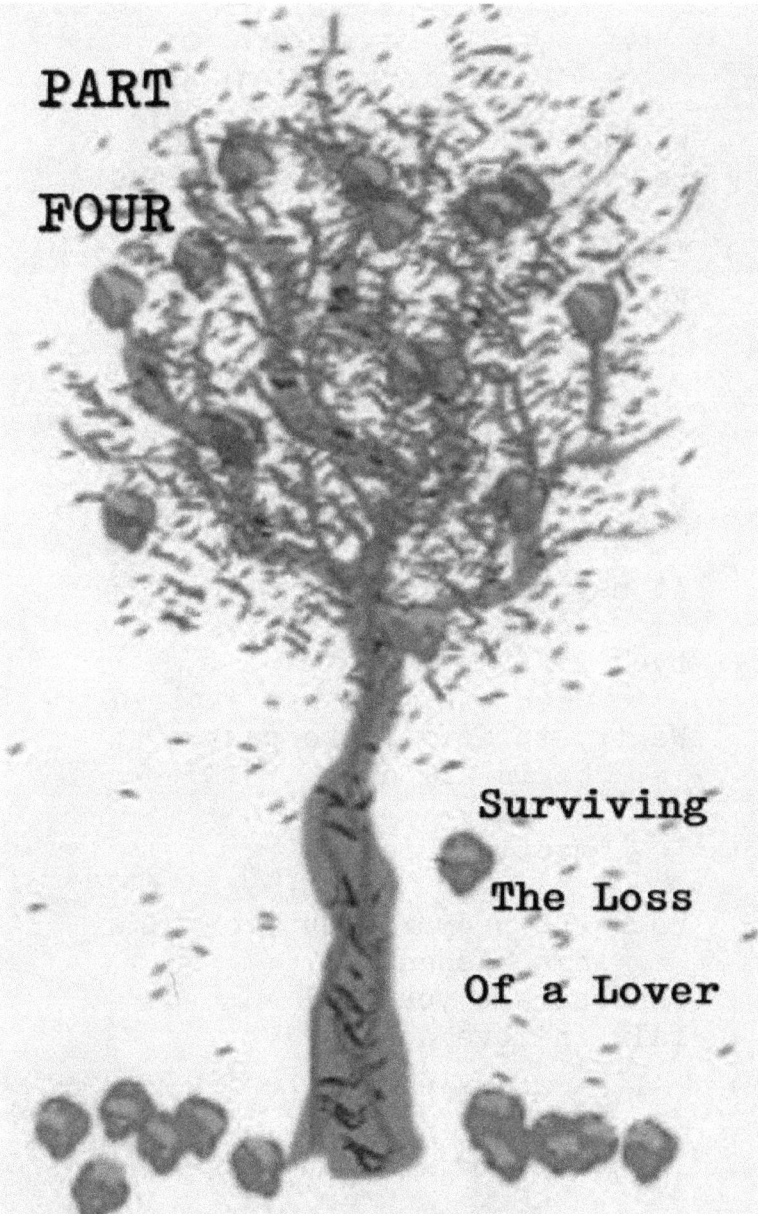

# PART

# FOUR

## Surviving

## The Loss

## Of a Lover

Jim Wortham

We have all loved
We have been hurt when the one
      we love left us
Time is a healer
We can speed the recovery
      by seeing good movies
      visiting friends
      use our emotions
            to paint pictures
            to write poems
Most relationships do not last

It may be difficult to learn
      to kiss a relationship good-
bye
      when its time has expired
We try to forget the past
      begin all over
      go out
      meet new people

When the proper amount of time
      has passed
chances are you will
fall in love again

## <u>VULNERABLE</u>

Good people
are often
vulnerable

I have been honest
about my love for you
how I crave your care
how I want your love

I have laid myself
before you
like a mirror
You can wreck me
or build me up

I
am
vulnerable

Jim Wortham

## <u>DO YOU WANT ME?</u>

Perhaps it is not having you
or
not being sure
where I stand with you
that causes my love
to be so strong

Maybe if everything
were all right
I could be the one
questioning whether you
are good enough for me

But I am on the ground
looking up at you
Do you want me
?

Say

"YES"

## INFATUATION

You brought
too many happy times
to my life
for me to forget you

I cannot
turn my love
off
as you did

Your love was not true love
It did not last
It was infatuation only

I did not lose love
I never had it
I only lost your
infatuation
which I did not want
anyway

Jim Wortham

## <u>TOO MUCH</u>

Why do you
have to be
the one who says
goodbye
?

Why can't
we part
as friends
while feeling
the same love
?

I love you
too much
to be your friend
You like
me too much
to be my lover

## WHY?

You were first
    to say
  I love you

You were first
    to say
    goodbye
    to love

    I stand
    hurting

wondering why
you had to say either

Jim Wortham

## <u>REALITY</u>

The idea of someday
coming home to a weekend
and being alone
has become a painful reality

I sometimes thought
and laughed
What would I do
if that ever happened
?

I am asking myself
tonight
What do I do
now that it has happened
?

## <u>LOVE WILL COME</u>

Count the days
(I tell myself)
and the pain
will be gone soon

The pain becomes
less intense
each day

One day
(soon I hope)
someone beautiful
will come into
my life

Then
I tell myself
that love
is here to last...

(again)

81

Jim Wortham

# <u>LOVE ONCE KNEW OUR NAMES</u>

There was a time
we spent all day
everyday together

You told all your friends
how you found love
You showed me
to all of them

We spend whole evenings
laughing
talking and touching
studying for tests
going to fancy theaters
enjoying the swings in the park
eating at a pizza palace

We spent our days
and evenings
together
All of them

## SONGS

I like
laying on the floor
listening to
sad songs

My friends
are all
with dates

I play sad records
not happy ones
Happy songs
are
out of place

Jim Wortham

## I NEED MEMORIES

Some day
I will realize
our love
has
ended

But today
perhaps tomorrow
I
still
need
its
memories

## ONCE UPON A TIME

Once upon a time
we did have a chance together
We were teenagers
walking in a park
We had seen each other at school
Why was I so afraid to ask your name
?

We were afraid of rejection
At least I was
Maybe I was and you were not
You were beautiful
I was shy

You said you always wondered
what would have happened
if we had gotten together
way back then

I have wondered too

Jim Wortham

# <u>THURSDAY</u>

It is Thursday
It is night
It is raining
The sounds of blowing wind
     train whistles
     sloshing cars
     enter my room
as I sit thinking
How you once laughed and smiled
How you once knew me

It is hard for me to believe
that I did not think
I would miss you

This is not the first time
probably will not be the last
because it seems
I really do not know
how much I love someone
until I am without her

If I had a chance
with her again
I would never be unkind
to her
But there would still be
some reason
why we would not
be together
for long

Jim Wortham

# I AIN'T CRYING THE BLUES

Looking back
to my youth
I gave my days and nights
to work
and to writing poems

All the time
wanting to be a writer
and live off the poems
I wrote and wrote
for years

It is strange
how time slips by slowly
Now the wind is blowing
a different direction
I realized my dream
of writing was nothing
more than a dream

I stopped looking
for the dream

I ain't crying the blues
just
thinking things through

Jim Wortham

# WE STOPPED SHARING

We shared
a lot of things

Once
we were happy

You started
looking around
to see who else
was near

I do not remember
when you started
sharing
less and less with me
and more with others

I just know
somewhere
you ran ahead of me
and we
stopped sharing

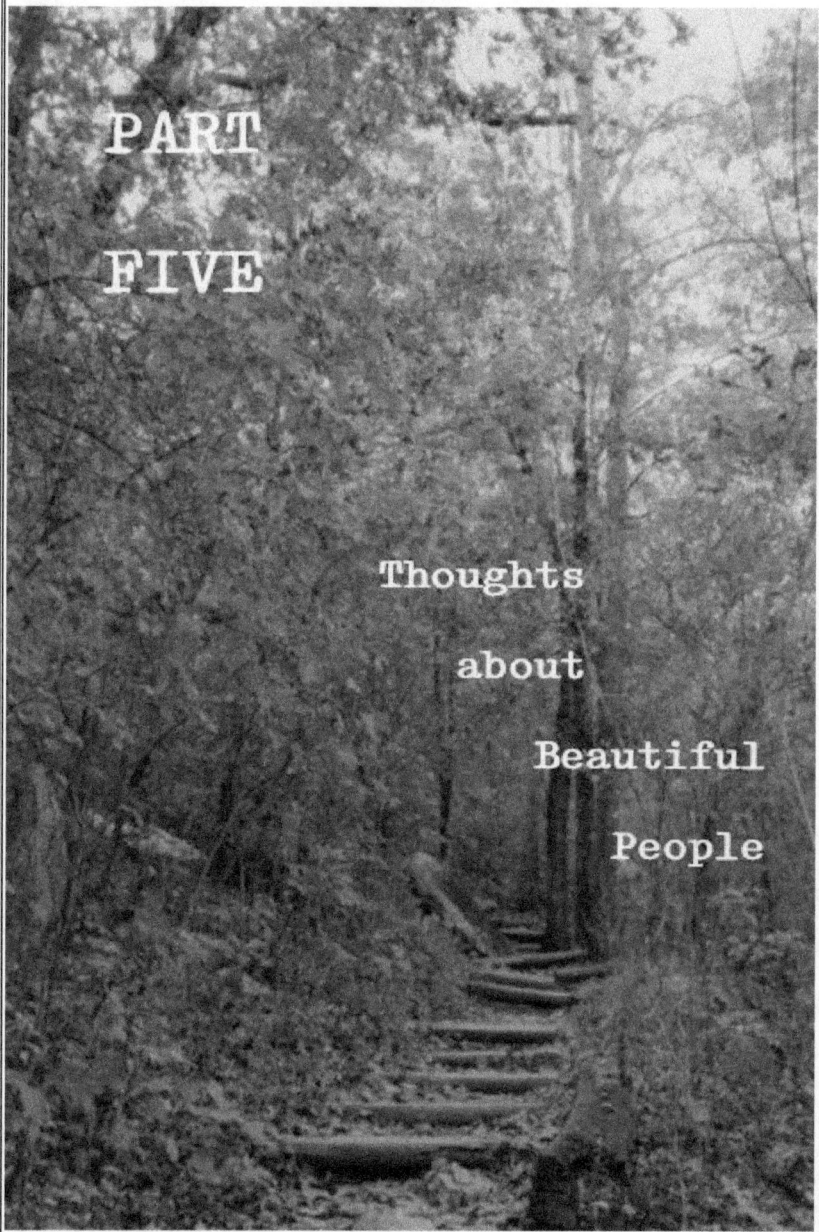

# PART

# FIVE

Thoughts

about

Beautiful

People

Jim Wortham

# DEAR LADY

Dear Lady
the sophistication
you learned from others
has built a mask
that guards you
The mask has destroyed
the freedom to be yourself
hasn't it
?

Does the voice
inside you
scream for something
simple
real
?

As much as you try
to reject it
is there a desire to live
beyond high words
and don't-touch-me-symbols
?

## <u>WHEN I MET YOU</u>

My mind

used to picture

what life would

be like

if I had someone

I could love


All those pictures

became real

Jim Wortham

## <u>INNER BEAUTY</u>

I have grown
into
knowing you

As I did

your inner beauty
became
more beautiful

# I WILL SURVIVE

I held her
during the
speeding moments
toward her death

The moment
came
Our eyes locked

Then she was
gone

Jim Wortham

## <u>AFTERWARDS</u>

I tried
to rearrange
my life
after her
death

It is hard
but time
is a healer

I will survive
One day
I will look up
and see
the sun shine
once again

## TWO LOVERS

When two lovers
are together
it is amusing to see
how one of them
will bring up
a silly idea
to see the other react
Then they both laugh

Days later
the same silly idea
is mentioned again
This time
in a serious manner

Jim Wortham

## NANCY

It is all right
for her to be
cold
insensitive

       Others
       made her that way
       Once she trusted
       Once she loved

People
gave her reasons
to be afraid

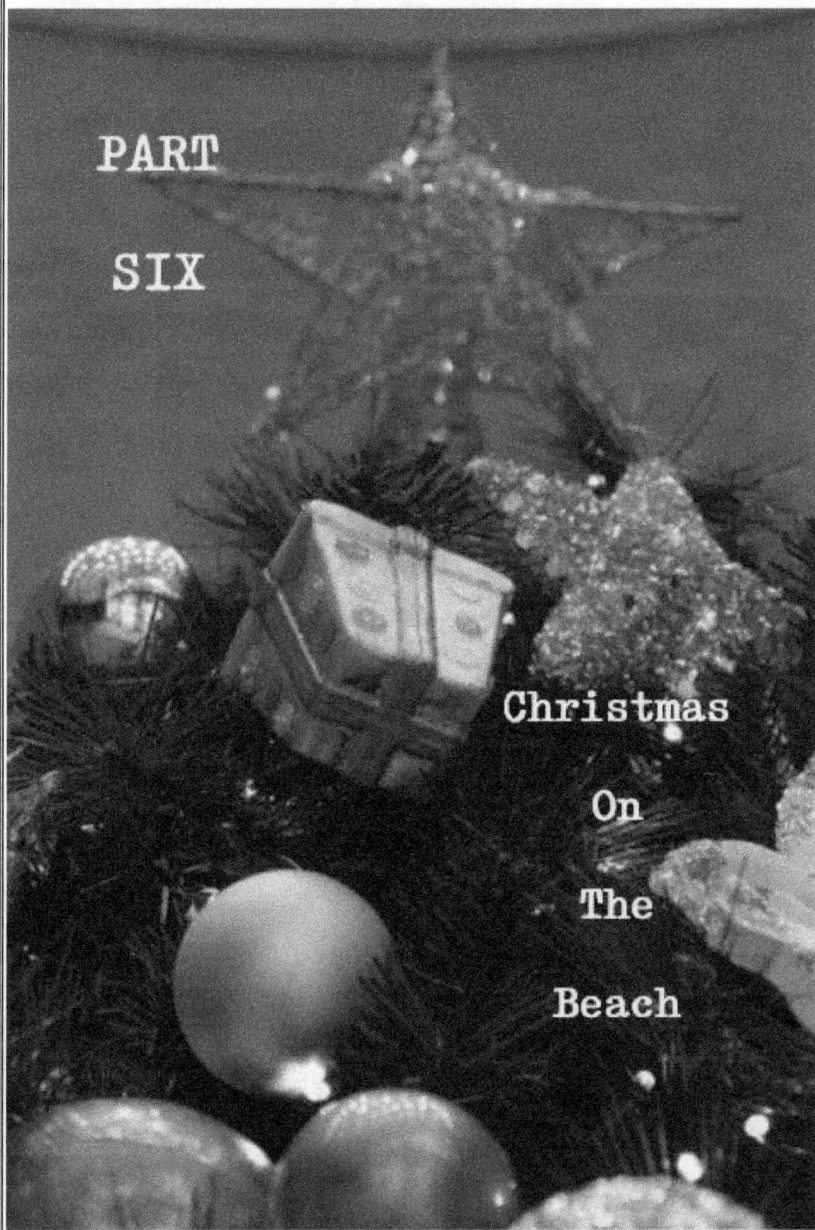

PART

SIX

Christmas

On

The

Beach

Jim Wortham

# RETURN TO THE BEACH

I love the beach
    the breeze
    the sand under my toes
    splashing waves
        inspire me

As I get older
I enjoy going to the beach
alone
less and less
There is a need for
someone
to share happy times

Last Christmas
I went to the beach
alone
It felt empty
    no children
    no older couples
    no one my age

I felt alone

## EMPTY BEACH

The beach
is
empty

I walk
the white sands
hoping
to meet
another lonely person

Maybe
we can become
friends

Jim Wortham

# <u>JUST SEARCHING</u>

On the beach
I pass motels
stopping at each
looking around the pools
hoping to find
someone
to share Christmas

A girl sitting on
a lawn chair
says 'Hi"
We talk a little
then she wants
to be alone
again

She was just being friendly
She did not want to talk
long

But I want
someone
to spend Christmas with

## <u>MUSIC</u>

Beside a pool
at a beautiful motel
background music
keeps me company

Music is not as nice
as a person
but music
is better than
being alone

Jim Wortham

# <u>FOOTSTEPS</u>

Walking to my motel
it occurred to me
this was going to be
an empty night

I heard footsteps
following me
I felt a bit of hope
I stopped and turned
to see who it was

It was the footsteps
of loneliness
following me
to my motel room

# COLD

Cold wind
blows through
window cracks
in my motel room

It is Christmas Eve
Time is slowing down
to make this
another
long
lonely night

The cold wind
the clock
and I
sit alone
on this Christmas Eve

Jim Wortham

## NIGHT

It is Christmas night
alone
Sometimes magazines
television
books
cannot kill
a lonely night

I would treat myself
to a fancy restaurant
but I don't have enough
money

## A SAD NEW YEAR'S EVE

The old man
drinking beer
wanted to talk
about his
long haired
drug addicted son
The old man
had told his son
not to return home
until he cut his hair
shaved
got off drugs
The son is afraid to go home

The old man
drinking beer
tears running from his eyes
secretly told me
that he would welcome
his son with open arms
if only
he would come home

Jim Wortham

## <u>DANCING</u>

Do you remember

dancing

on the beach

where eyes

and feelings spoke

?

That night

became a snapshot

I look at

often


Years have passed

Do you remember

dancing

?

## <u>TO KAREN</u>

It is New Year's Eve
There is no party this year
No laughter
No one

So I relax
in my motel room
thinking about
last New Year's Eve
when I was at a party
where our eyes met
hands touched

Distance has kept up apart
Summer will bring you
closer to me

It is New Year's Eve
There is no party this year
No laughter
So I fill these moments
with thoughts
of you

Jim Wortham

## I AM COMING HOME

Friends
I miss
your acceptance of me

I miss
you calling
wanting to be
with me

Friends
I will be
home
soon

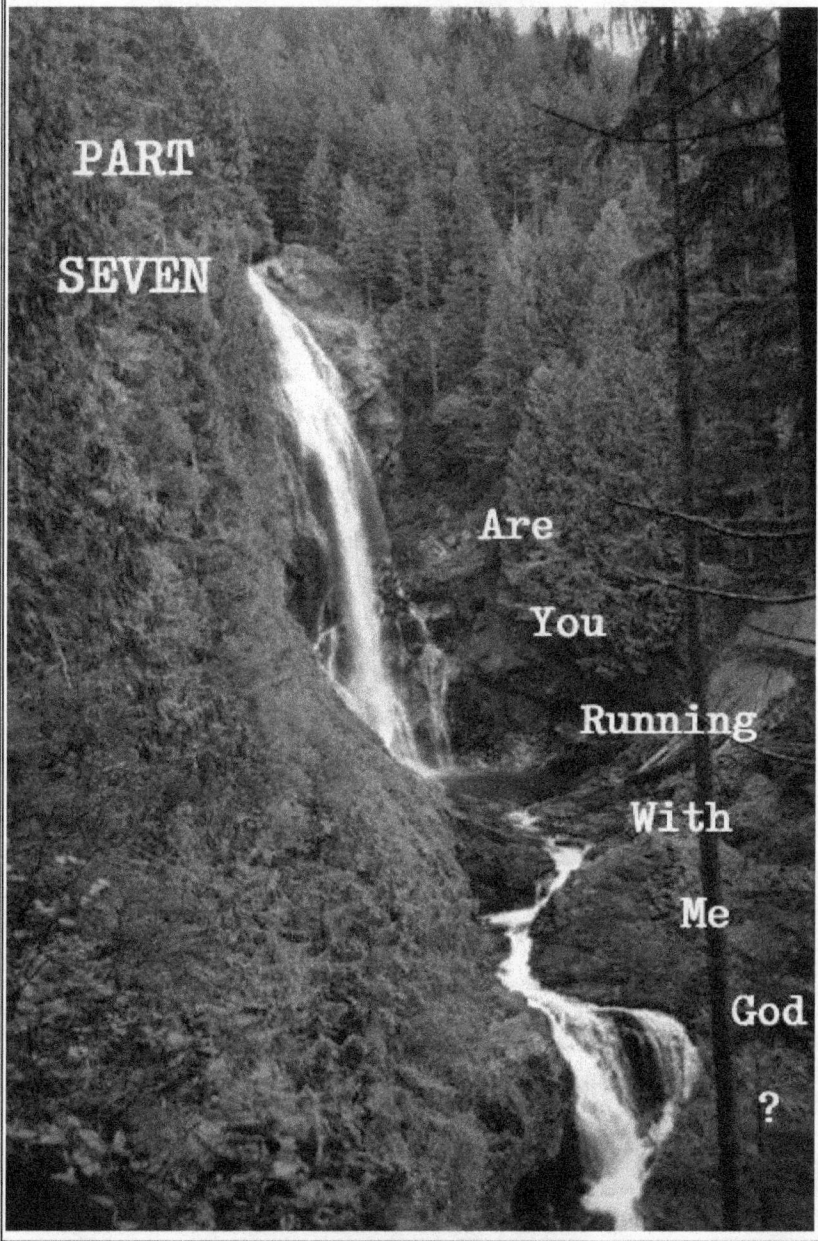

PART

SEVEN

Are

You

Running

With

Me

God

?

Jim Wortham

Every sensitive person I know
has contact with God from time
to time.  Someone may say they are
inspired, or feel especially
happy and thrilled for no
particular reason, or has a
great idea.

This is communication with God.

As I drift away from the simple
life, I lose my close contact with
and guidance from God.  As I get
too busy, I neglect listening to
Him.

Here are a few poems I wrote to
help
you see another side of me.

# I THINK I AM GOING TO FAIL MY EXAM

I close my eyes
but sleep will not come
I am worried about
the exam tomorrow
the term paper due Friday

I think I am going to
fail my test
I did not keep up
the reading assignments
I delayed reviewing
until this afternoon
I always do this
always put things off
until the last moment
I am always ashamed
to pray
when
I did not do my part

Jim Wortham

# <u>IT IS HEAVY</u>
*(me talking to Jesus)*

Dear Jesus
the guilt is heavy
A Christian told me
it was okay to smoke
to drink
to tell off-color jokes
as long as it was done
in moderation

So I picked up all these habits
Tonight
I feel the guilt
It is coming down heavy
I cannot sleep
I am restless
Let me start over
Jesus
Please

## I LOVE YOU
### (Jesus talking to me)

I love you
just as you are
with your
      hang-ups
      bad habits
      mixed- up world

I love you this way
I am waiting
for the moment
when you realize this

Come to me
Drop your bad habits
Accept my love

Jim Wortham

## <u>SOMEONE TO LOVE</u>

Dear Jesus
thank you for sending me
someone to love

You heard me praying
for someone
with whom to share
    my thoughts
     simple times
She brings out the best
in me
She accepts me
as I am

Help me
to love her
Let me bring out
the best in her

## PRAYERS AND PROMISES

Walking along the beach
you and I
stop
to offer
silent prayers

Giving thanks
for having met

Jim Wortham

## <u>IN MY ROOM</u>

I have heard
you can look into a person's eyes
and see their soul
One can see sadness
madness
love
sometimes even evil

I have seen or felt
most of these
feelings and longings
I may have avoided harm
by identifying evil
in a person's eyes

I am lucky
I believe God's angels
surround me at all times

Being kind to each person
offering hope
when needed
I have been unharmed
I have prayed for protection

I do not have the answers
I do not claim to have answers
to why evil happens in the world

I do know that with
God's angels
surrounding me
I am protected

Jim Wortham

# PRASERS HANGING FROM HEAVEN

I have sent a lot
of prayers
up there

Over the years
many prayers
did not seem to be answered
I am glad
they were not

Many prayers
were self-centered
would have been
destructive to me

Those prayers were answered
in silence
another word for NO
or NOT NOW

Looking over the years
YES
prayers
worked for my good
Others could have taken me
down the wrong path

Life has been good

Jim Wortham

## THE WINDOW

I watch
my prayers
leave the bedroom window
hang from stars
like colorful flowers
I feel certain
by morning
that they will be
answered

Can prayers
make tomorrow
beautiful
again
?

PART

EIGHT

A

Poet

Is

Born

The road to getting published
and promoted is very difficult.
No one wants to help an unknown
poet, so I had to help myself.

My friends helped as I began
climbing the tall ladder to
success.  I still have a long
way to go to get where I want
to be.

In Part Eight, I will sketch a
few days in my life as a poet.

## THIS IS HOW IT HAPPENED

One night
friends got high
on oven roasted pizza
and cola
I read them my poems

They liked my poems
pooled their money
so I could print
my poetry
in book form

I visited bookstores
in big cities
showed them my books
Bookstores began
selling them

Jim Wortham

# THE SIMPLE LIFE

Writing is a simple life
Writing took me back to
simpler ways

I took time
to watch the stars
take walks in the park

I began to talk
to God again
like I did as a child
I always listened
to see if God would say
something
to me

# WRITING POETRY

I wrote more poems
compiled new books
At first
books were slow to sell
I almost starved
but my friends
took care of me

Once when I was penniless
without food
I walked in the village
When I came back
to my apartment
I found groceries on my table
and ten dollars
No note
I do not know who left them

Jim Wortham

## <u>TIME PASSED</u>

Two years passed
I lived penny to penny
day to day

I kept writing
praying
that someday my books
would become popular
I prayed in the mornings
asking Jesus to help me
make a living
from my books
I also prayed at night
Jesus helped me stretch
my pennies to buy things
He sent friends along to help

## INVITED TO A PARTY

I was invited to a party and was
asked to read my poems.  As I
read, a girl looked at me, I
looked back into her eyes. Our
eyes spoke the same language.

We began a new love
relationship.  It is still
going on, and I hope it will
last.

Jim Wortham

## DREAMS

Now it seems
my dreams
have come true

I am not rich
I have enough to eat
I can buy gas for my car
I am not late paying rent
I even opened a savings account
I put a dollar into it each week
I am not famous
I have people who write me
      after reading my books
We touch each other's lives
      through letters

I talk with God more now
He always listens
Sometimes I hear Him
speaking with the silence
of my thoughts

## <u>LIFE</u>

What more can I ask
of life
?

I am
content

I love
life

Jim Wortham

## The Seasons of Love Series

The Summer of Love     $ 9.95

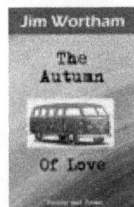

The Autumn of Love     $ 9.95

The Winter of Love     $ 9.95

The Spring of Love     $ 9.95

Thank you for reading my book.
Autographed copies are available from
Jim Wortham, PO Box 40
Madison, Indiana  47250-0040 U.S.A.
Email:  Jim Wortham123@gmail.com

Shipping within the United States is
$5 for the entire order.  Contact me
for overseas shipping costs.

## Follow Jim Wortham

Jim's blog: www.JimWorthamPoet.com
Facebook: www.facebook.com/Jim.Wortham.54
Jim's email: jimwortham123@gmail.com

Jim Wortham Poetry Books
Post Office Box 40
Madison, Indiana 47250-0040
U.S.A.

*Autographed books available*

www.ingramcontent.com/pod-product-compliance
Lightning Source LLC
Chambersburg PA
CBHW031516040426
42445CB00009B/259